THE OFFICIAL

BIRMINGHAM CITY

ANNUAL 2022

Written by **Rob Mason**
Designed by **Marek Ludwiczak**

A Grange Publication

© 2021. Published by Grange Communications Ltd., Edinburgh, under licence from Birmingham City Football Club. Printed in the EU.

Photographs © Birmingham City Football Club & PA Images; with thanks to Roy

CONTENTS

CAN YOU MANAGE?

Fancy being Blues boss? How is your football knowledge?
Test yourself and find the answers on page 61.

BLUES BOSSES

How well do you know these Blues bosses? Can you write which country each of these managers is from below their picture?

Alex McLeish   **Pep Clotet**   **Lee Bowyer**

_____   _____   _____

WHO PLAYS WHERE?

Birmingham City will play at all of the following stadiums in 2021-22 but which teams will they face? Write in the name of the club who play at each stadium.

Bloomfield Road   **Craven Cottage**   **The Riverside Stadium**   **The Hawthorns**   **The New Den**

_____   _____   _____   _____   _____

EYE-DENTITY

Can you look these Blues players in the eyes and work out who is who?

_____   _____   _____   _____   _____

INTERNATIONAL BREAK

Which countries can call up these players when it is on international break?
Write the name of the country next to the player. The countries these players represent are
Australia, Croatia, Denmark, Philippines and Republic of Ireland, but who plays for who?

Neil Etheridge	Kristian Pedersen	Ivan Sunjic	Riley McGree	Scott Hogan
_____	_____	_____	_____	_____

WHO SCORED?

Do you know who scored these important goals?

1. Both goals in April's important 2-1 win at Derby in 2021?

_____

2. The winner in January's 1-0 win at Middlesbrough, also in 2021?

_____

3. The brilliant goal against Sheffield Wednesday in a key promotion game in April 2007 when he ran from the half-way line to score the goal of the season?

_____

4. The first goal in the 2011 League Cup final?

_____

5. The winner against Arsenal in the 2011 League Cup final?

_____

PLAYER OF THE YEAR
DEAN'S DOUBLE

Inspirational skipper Harlee Dean won both the Supporters' Player of the Year and the Players' Player of the Year awards in the summer of 2021.

Dean's central defensive partner Marc Roberts and top scorer Lukas Jutkiewicz also took top three places in the fans' award, while Maxime Colin and Ivan Sanchez featured strongly in the votes from the players.

It is not the first time Dean has had a Player of the Year award to take home. When he was with Brentford he collected the Supporters' Player of the Year in 2017, while in 2013 he shared the Bees Players' Player of the Year award with Simon Moore.

Last season Dean played in 43 of the 46 Championship fixtures, scoring winners at Bristol City and Rotherham United, and another to earn a point at Stoke City. He also scored in a home victory over Reading. Only Lukas Jutkiewicz and Scott Hogan scored more than Dean but it was his ability to stop goals rather than score them that was the main reason for his success.

Man of the Match in three live Sky games, Dean won 38% of the votes in the supporters' poll. Always ready to speak his mind, the captain is a born leader. His spirit and organisational skills were vital as he dominated in defence as, under Lee Bowyer, Blues finished the season strongly.

An experienced player who turned 30 just before the start of the 2021-22 season, Dean was born in Basingstoke in Hampshire. He began his career with Dagenham & Redbridge, debuting in League Two against Port Vale on Halloween in 2009. It could have been a nightmare start as the Daggers were trailing when he came off the bench with nine minutes to go, but Dean hit the headlines immediately by setting up Scott Doe's late equaliser for his side.

However, Dean never played for the club again! He went out on loan five times before signing for Southampton but he never got a game despite being on the bench three times. From the Saints, he went on loan to Bishops Stortford, but it was when he then went on loan to Brentford in 2011 that Dean started to be able to show what he could do.

He played 249 games for Brentford before coming to Birmingham City in 2017 and needs to play just 31 times in 2021-22 to reach 200 appearances for Blues.

BLUES GREATS
TREVOR FRANCIS

BIRMINGHAM CITY

TREVOR FRANCIS

As lightning fast as any footballer you could ever wish to see.

His speed off the mark was incredible.

Just 16 years old when he made his debut for Birmingham City as a substitute at Cardiff City on 5 September 1970.

Scored on his first start.

Scored 15 goals in his first 16 games.

Became the first 16-year-old to score four goals in a top flight game when Birmingham beat Bolton 4-0 two months before his 17th birthday.

Won promotion with Birmingham in 1972.

Scored 25 top-flight goals and another couple in the FA Cup in 1977-78.

Reached the FA Cup semi-final with Blues in 1972 and 1975.

Scored 133 times for Birmingham in 329 appearances.

Scored 282 goals in 783 games in his career.

Became Britain's first £1m footballer.

Scored the only goal of the 1979 European Cup final for Nottingham Forest v Malmo of Sweden.

Played in the USA with Detroit, in Italy with Sampdoria and Atalanta, and Scotland with Rangers, as well as playing for Manchester City and Sheffield Wednesday.

Scored 12 goals in 52 games for England.

Returned to St. Andrew's as manager in May 1996.

Took Birmingham to three play-offs and the 2001 League Cup final, only to lose on penalties to Liverpool.

Also managed QPR, Sheffield Wednesday (see above photograph) and Crystal Palace.

SPOT THE DIFFERENCE

Here's a challenge for you... Can you spot **10 differences** between the two images below?

Find out the answers on page 61.

FACT OR FIB?

Some of these statements about Blues are true - but some are made up.
Can you work out which are facts and which are fibs?

		FACT	FIB
1)	Birmingham were league champions in 1931.		
2)	Birmingham – or Small Heath as they were called then – were the first ever Second Division champions?		
3)	On both occasions they have won the League Cup, Blues have knocked out Aston Villa.		
4)	A player called Bradford is Blues' highest ever goal-scorer.		
5)	A player called Halifax is Blues' second highest ever goal-scorer.		
6)	The only manager to lead England to World Cup final victory also managed Blues.		
7)	The first ever substitute to score a hat-trick was Birmingham's Geoff Vowden.		
8)	On their way to a war-time game at Luton in 1940, the Blues' team bus crashed into a traffic island because a 'black-out' meant the driver couldn't see.		
9)	When Blues were the opposition for Arsenal's first ever FA Cup tie in 1892, the kick-off was delayed by 25 minutes because the referee got lost.		
10)	Birmingham were founder members of the Premier League.		
11)	Lukas Jutkiewicz has been Blues' top scorer for the last three seasons.		
12)	Trevor Francis was the first player to be sold by Blues for £2m.		
13)	Blues' best ever League Cup win was against Manchester United.		
14)	A gigantic crowd of over 66,000 is Blues' record attendance.		
15)	Blues have played Barcelona, Inter Milan and Roma in European competition.		
16)	Blues have played Bayern Munich, AC Milan and Ajax in European competition.		
17)	Trevor Francis won more England caps while with Birmingham than any other player.		
18)	David Dunn is the most expensive English player Blues have ever bought.		
19)	Blues sold Che Adams to AFC Bournemouth in 2019.		
20)	Lee Bowyer played for England.		

Find out the answers on page 61.

SPOT THE SEASON

A test for your Blues knowledge! Using the clues provided,
do you think you can figure out what season is being described? Is it:

2008-09, 2009-10, 2010-11 or 2011-12

1 Birmingham City beat Arsenal 2-1 in the League Cup final.

2 Ben Foster, Curtis Davies and Nikola Zigic were amongst the new signings.

3 The team were relegated, finishing 18th in the Premier League.

4 Aston Villa were beaten in the quarter-final at St. Andrew's.

5 The Blues also reached the quarter-finals of the FA Cup.

6 Lee Bowyer was a key member of the Blues midfield and scored in the League Cup semi-final, as West Ham were beaten.

7 Craig Gardner was top scorer in all competitions with 10 goals.

8 Stephen Carr, Roger Johnson and Ben Foster were ever-present in the Premier League.

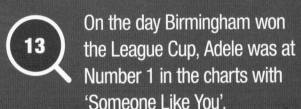

9 Alex McLeish was manager.

10 Obafemi Martins scored the winning goal in the League Cup final in the 89th minute, six minutes after coming on as a sub.

11 Winning the League Cup meant Birmingham qualified for Europe.

12 Manchester United won the Premier League and Manchester City won the FA Cup.

13 On the day Birmingham won the League Cup, Adele was at Number 1 in the charts with 'Someone Like You'.

Find the answer on page 61

CELEBRITY FANS

Birmingham City have many famous fans including stars from the music, film and TV worlds. Look out for these Bluenoses and Keep Right On when you see them.

JAMES PHELPS

Fred Weasley in the Harry Potter films.

ADAM ZINDANI

Rhythm guitarist with the Stereophonics.

STEVEN KNIGHT

Film director behind the Peaky Blinders TV series set in the Small Heath area of Birmingham, Small Heath Alliance being Birmingham City's original name. Steven Knight was also one of the creators of the gameshow, 'Who Wants To Be A Millionaire?'

JASPER CARROTT

Very famous TV comedian and former Birmingham City director who once had a hit record with a song called 'Funky Moped' which was produced by Jeff Lynne.

GLYNN PURNELL

TV chef who is a massive Blues fan.
A presenter of 'Saturday Kitchen' on the BBC, his Birmingham restaurant has a Michelin Star.

DAVID HAREWOOD

Star of Homeland who has been in many TV shows from Dr. Who to being a guest host on Have I Got News For You? He saved two penalties as England goalkeeper at the 2018 Soccer Aid which raised more than £5m for UNICEF.

JEFF LYNNE

Musical Megastar whose Mr. Blue Sky is part of the St. Andrew's soundtrack. Lynne is leader of the Electric Light Orchestra and member of the super-group The Travelling Wilburys.

ROY WOOD

The singer and writer of 'I Wish It Could Be Christmas Every Day', who was behind the hugely successful bands 'The Move' (who were the first band ever played on Radio 1), Electric Light Orchestra' (with Jeff Lynne) and Wizzard.

COLIN BUCHANAN

Star of Dalziel and Pascoe where he plays DI Peter Pascoe.

SIMON FOWLER
OF OCEAN COLOUR SCENE

A keen Birmingham fan, as is Ocean Colour Scene guitarist Andy Bennett.

UB40

Birmingham based reggae band with more than 50 hits to their name who even sent a good luck message to the Blues from their tour bus while on an American tour.

MIKE SKINNER
OF THE STREETS

Having been brought up in the West Heath area of Birmingham, Mike wrote of his support for Birmingham City in his autobiography.

MARTIN SAUNDERS
OF THE TWANG

A Bluenose whose favourite player was France international centre-forward Christophe Dugarry.

SEASON REVIEW

The 2020-21 season started with some optimism around St. Andrew's after the arrival of Aitor Karanka as head coach and a host of new signings including **Jon Toral**, who had been Blues Player of the Year when on loan from Arsenal in 2015-16, George Friend and Adam Clayton from one of Karanka's old clubs Middlesbrough,

wingers **Ivan Sanchez** from Spanish football and Jonathan Leko from near neighbours West Brom as well as agile goalkeeper **Neil Etheridge** from Cardiff City.

When further signings came in after an opening day league victory over the previous season's play-off finalists Brentford, things were looking up. Bluenoses knew all about **Scott Hogan** who was signed from Aston Villa. Fans hoped he'd get off to the sort of blistering start he had when coming to St. Andrew's on loan earlier in the year when he plundered seven goals in his first nine games. When Hogan was speedily joined by Spain international **Mikel San Jose**, a veteran of almost 400 games for Athletic Bilbao alongside the acquisition of 'one for the future' Oriol Soldevila from Barcelona, it appeared that Karanka was assembling a blend of youth and experience.

Three draws that followed the beating of the Bees seemed like a steady start, especially as Karanka's reputation for establishing a solid defence had seen only two goals leaked in the first four games. Although there had also been a disappointing 1-0 loss to Cambridge United in the Carabao Cup before the Championship kicked off, there was some hope that Blues would at least improve on the previous season's 20th place and just possibly make a push for the play-offs.

By late October those hopes had faded as one draw from three games had extended the winless run to six games. However, back-to-back victories at home to Huddersfield and away to Preston fired Aitor's aces into the top half of the table to renew hope.

This would become the pattern of the season: odd glimmers of optimism amongst too many lengthy winless runs. After the victory at Deepdale, courtesy of **Gary Gardner's** late winner, only three points were taken from the next six winless fixtures before another back to back blast, this time with consecutive away wins at promotion chasing Bristol City and Reading. **Harlee Dean** scored a late winner at Ashton Gate but was then sent off at the Madejski Stadium where a brace from Jon-Miquel Toral made him the hero. At this point Blues were 15th; 10 points clear of the drop zone but eight shy of the play-offs.

By Christmas Day, three defeats in a row, including a 4-1 home loss to Middlesbrough, left Karanka frustrated at losing to an old club, although there was better news on Boxing Day with a goalless draw at the head coach's most recent club Nottingham Forest. Two more defeats then preceded a trip to Manchester City in the FA Cup. When Pep Guardiola named a strong side including Ruben Dias, Phil Foden, Kevin De Bruyne, Gabriel Jesus and Riyad Mahrez it looked like an uphill battle, especially as the home side raced into a 3-0 lead by the 33rd minute, but that proved the final score as Blues battled on.

The response was a strong one as Birmingham then went to Middlesbrough and delighted Karanka with a Scott Hogan goal sealing a 1-0 win. Once again it was a glimmer of optimism amongst a losing run. Victory at Boro was the only win in 14 league and cup games from early December to mid-February when a 1-0 win at struggling Sheffield Wednesday was one of two that sandwiched a defeat to leaders Norwich. The defeat to the Canaries left Blues looking over their shoulder just one place and two points above third bottom Rotherham who had two games in hand.

By mid-March and a 3-0 home loss to Bristol City, that gap to Rotherham had increased to three points, but by now the Millers had four games in hand of fourth bottom Blues and the board acted: Karanka left the club to be replaced by **Lee Bowyer** who was given ten games to guide Birmingham to safety. The former Blues and England midfielder had resigned as Charlton Athletic manager a day before being appointed at St. Andrew's where he brought fresh ideas and new energy.

Goals from **Lukas Jutkiewicz** and Harlee Dean brought a Bowyer bounce as the double was done over Reading. Under Karanka the longest unbeaten run of the season had been three draws, but after losing away to eventually promoted Watford in his second game, new boss Bowyer produced a great six-match run of four wins and two draws to guarantee Championship football with two games to go. No goals were conceded in the first four of those games in a run which included 1-0 wins over play-off finalists Swansea and away to a Rotherham side who had kept Blues in their sights.

A final place of 18th saw Blues nine points clear of the drop and level on points with 17th placed Nottingham Forest. It had been a long hard campaign but the form shown at the business end under Bowyer meant that while it had not been a good season it had ended well and 2021-22 could be looked forward to with the hope that this time the optimism would not be misplaced.

STAT ATTACK

- Lukas Jutkiewicz top scored with eight goals.
- Ivan Sanchez contributed seven assists with Jeremie Bela managing six.
- Blues averaged 48% possession at home and 45% away.
- Blues had five penalties awarded but 10 given against.
- Blues' away record was the joint 11th best in the division.
- Automatic promotion winners Watford won just two more away points than Blues.
- Only relegated Rotherham took fewer points at home.
- Other than a 2-0 home win over Stoke City, all of Blues other 12 victories were by one goal.
- Harlee Dean, Ivan Sunjic and Neil Etheridge each appeared in 43 of the 46 Championship games.
- Maxime Colin played in all but four league games as did Lukas Jutkiewicz, but 17 of the top-scorer's 42 appearances were as a substitute.
- Ivan Sanchez appeared 40 times.
- 34 players played in the Championship for Birmingham City.

GOALKEEPERS

1 NEIL ETHERIDGE

Birthplace:	**London**
Birthdate:	**7 February 1990**
2020-21 appearances:	**43**
2020-21 clean sheets:	**13**
Previous clubs:	**Chelsea, Fulham, Leatherhead (L), Charlton Athletic (L), Bristol Rovers (L), Crewe Alexandra (L), Oldham Athletic, Charlton Athletic, Walsall, Cardiff City.**
International:	**England Under 16s, Philippines**

A very experienced keeper with over 60 caps for the Philippines, Etheridge was Footballer of the Year there in 2018; a season in which he also helped Cardiff City to promotion to the Premier League. The following year he was ever-present in the Premier League before moving from the Bluebirds to Blues. An academy player with Chelsea, initially as a forward, Etheridge made his first team debut in the Europa League with Fulham.

MATIJA SARKIC 13

Birthplace:	**Grimsby**
Birthdate:	**23 July 1997**
2020-21 appearances:	**29**
2020-21 clean sheets:	**0**
Previous clubs:	**Anderlecht, Aston Villa, Wigan Athletic (L), Stratford Town (L), Havant & Waterlooville (L), Livingston (L), Wolves, Shrewsbury Town (L)**

On loan for the season from Wolves, Matija is a Montenegro international who spent last season on loan to Shrewsbury Town. A keeper who likes to command his box, he joined Wolves on a three year deal from Aston Villa in 2020. Born in Grimsby, Sarkic's father Bojan is a diplomat who was Montenegro's ambassador to the European Union. With Neil Etheridge suffering with Covid-19, Sarkic was the regular Blues keeper in pre-season.

ZACH JEACOCK

38

Birthplace:	**Birmingham**
Birthdate:	**8 May 2001**
2020-21 appearances:	**2**
2020-21 clean sheets:	**1**
Previous clubs:	**Stourport Swifts (L), Gloucester City (L)**
International:	**England Under 19s**

Jeacock kept a clean sheet against promotion-bound Brentford on his debut last season and was given a second appearance at the end of the season against Cardiff City. Until the age of 14 he was an outfield player. A month after debuting for Blues, Jeacock played his first game for England Under 19s against Greece.

CONNAL TRUEMAN **27**

Birthplace:	**Birmingham**
Birthdate:	**26 March 1996**
2020-21 appearances:	**1**
2020-21 clean sheets:	**0**
Previous clubs:	**Leamington (L), Solihull Moors (L), AFC Wimbledon (L), Swindon Town (L)**

Trueman played 27 times last season: 22 times for AFC Wimbledon, four for Swindon and once for Blues at the end of the season away to Blackburn Rovers. He began the current campaign with 13 Championship appearances to his name for Blues.

DEFENDERS

12

HARLEE DEAN

Birthplace:	**Basingstoke**
Birthdate:	**26 July 1991**
2020-21 appearances:	**43 + 1**
2020-21 goals:	**4**
Previous clubs:	**Dagenham & Redbridge, Southampton, Brentford**

Blues' current Player of the Year, Harlee was twice Player of the Year at his previous club Brentford with whom he was a promotion winner in 2014. Although he spent two years with Southampton, Dean didn't play a first team game for the Saints.

MAXIME COLIN

2

Birthplace:	**Arras, France**
Birthdate:	**15 November 1991**
2020-21 appearances:	**41 + 3**
2020-21 goals:	**1**
Previous clubs:	**Anzin-Saint-Aubin, Arras, Vermelles, Avion, US Boulogne, Troyes, RSC Anderlecht, Brentford**
International:	**France Under 20**

French full-back Maxime Colin started out as a forward. He played for various clubs in France at youth level before breaking into first team football with Boulogne in 2010. He played Europa League football with famous Belgian club Anderlecht for whom he played in the 2015 Belgian Cup final before coming to English football with Brentford later that year. He signed for Blues in 2017.

KRISTIAN PEDERSEN

3

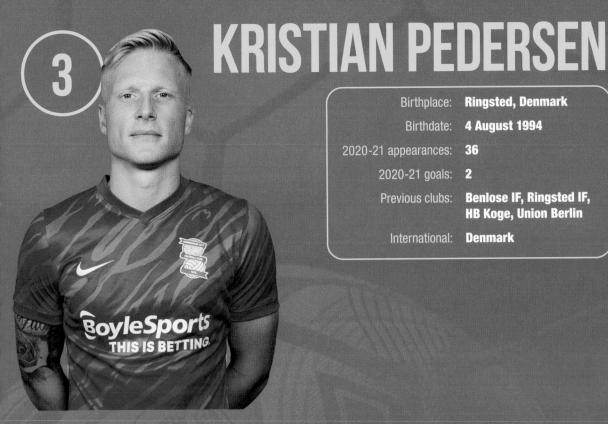

Birthplace:	**Ringsted, Denmark**
Birthdate:	**4 August 1994**
2020-21 appearances:	**36**
2020-21 goals:	**2**
Previous clubs:	**Benlose IF, Ringsted IF, HB Koge, Union Berlin**
International:	**Denmark**

6'2" left-back who can also play left midfield. After playing in his home country and in Germany, he came to Birmingham in the summer of 2018. Having won international honours at Under 21 level, Pedersen made his full international debut in October 2020 against the Faroe Islands.

MARC ROBERTS

4

Birthplace:	**Barnsley**
Birthdate:	**26 July 1990**
2020-21 appearances:	**29 + 8**
2020-21 goals:	**4**
Previous clubs:	**Wakefield, Worksop Town, Buxton, FC Halifax Town, Barnsley**
International:	**England C**

Capped at C (non-league) level by England, Roberts was 25 when he came into the Football League with his home town Barnsley who he went on to captain and win both promotion and the Football League Trophy in 2016. Particularly strong in the air, this centre-back joined Blues in 2017 and had made well over 100 appearances for the club by the start of the 2021-22 season.

GEORGE FRIEND

Birthplace:	**Barnstaple**
Birthdate:	**19 October 1987**
2020-21 appearances:	**23 + 5**
2020-21 goals:	**0**
Previous clubs:	**Exeter City, Wolves, Millwall (L), Southend Utd. (L), Scunthorpe Utd (L), Doncaster Rovers, Middlesbrough**

5

A promotion winner with Exeter, Wolves and Middlesbrough, and Player of the Year with Doncaster and Boro, Friend was also selected for the Championship Team of the Year in 2014-15 and 2015-16. In 2015 he gained a degree in sports journalism after doing a distance learning course with Staffordshire University.

DION SANDERSON

21

Birthplace:	**Wednesfield**
Birthdate:	**15 December 1999**
2020-21 appearances:	**20 + 7**
2020-21 goals:	**1**
Previous clubs:	**Wolves, Cardiff City (L), Sunderland (L)**

The nephew of Tessa Sanderson who won a gold medal in the javelin at the 1984 Olympics, Dion is so highly rated by his parent club Wolves that they gave him a new four year contract before entrusting him to Blues for a season long loan. It is Sanderson's third loan having reached the play-offs on his two previous loans to Cardiff City and Sunderland. Last season he won the Young Player of the Year award at Sunderland where he established himself in his preferred position of centre back after showing his versatility by impressing in both full-back positions.

JUAN CASTILLO

23

Birthplace:	**Amsterdam**
Birthdate:	**13 January 2000**
2020-21 appearances:	**18**
2020-21 goals:	**0**
Previous clubs:	**Ajax, Chelsea, AZ Alkmaar (L), ADO Den Haag (L)**
International:	**Netherlands Under 20**

On loan from Chelsea, Castillo has been capped by the Netherlands at every level from Under 15s to Under 20s. Last season he played once as a sub for AZ at Utrecht between Christmas and New Year after which he made nine Eredivisie starts for Den Haag plus seven more games as sub. He also played against Oxford United for Chelsea Under 21s in the Football League Trophy. He had scored against the same opposition on his first appearance in the competition in January 2018. Twice an FA Youth Cup winner he also reached two UEFA Youth League finals and will look to gain EFL experience with Birmingham this season.

NICO GORDON

50

MARCEL OAKLEY

52

Birthplace:	**Birmingham**
Birthdate:	**20 April 2002**
2020-21 appearances / goals:	**1 + 1 / 0**
Previous clubs:	**None**

Birthplace:	**Birmingham**
Birthdate:	**30 October 2002**
2020-21 appearances / goals:	**0 / 0**
Previous clubs:	**None**

A teenage Blues academy product who plays at centre-back but can also operate at full-back. Gordon made his first team debut in June 2020 against Hull City at St. Andrew's. He had four first team appearances to his name at the start of the 2021-22 season.

Oakley is a promising right-back who excels at getting forward and supporting the attack. He did so well since first coming into the Under 23 side for a 1-0 win at home to Derby County in February 2020 that in the summer of 2021 he was offered his first professional contract.

MIDFIELDERS

17

Birthplace:	**Campillo de Arenas, Spain**
Birthdate:	**23 September 1992**
2020-21 appearances:	**32 + 9**
2020-21 goals:	**2**
Previous clubs:	**Real Jaen, Atletico Madrid B, Almeria, Albacete, Elce**

IVAN SANCHEZ

The scorer of Blues' goal of the season at Cardiff City, Sanchez takes many of Blues' corner-kicks and is a tricky winger who always poses a threat. Before coming to Birmingham he played all of his football in Spain, helping Elche to promotion to La Liga.

IVAN SUNJIC

34

Birthplace:	**Zenica, Bosnia and Herzegovina**
Birthdate:	**9 October 1996**
2020-21 appearances:	**40 + 5**
2020-21 goals:	**0**
Previous clubs:	**Dinamo Zagreb, Lokomotiva**
International:	**Croatia**

Defensive midfielder who captained Croatia at the UEFA Under 21 European Championships in 2019 and who is a full international. Sunjic's experience also includes having played in the Europa League, winning the league title with Dinamo Zagreb and playing in the Croatian cup final.

GARY GARDNER

20

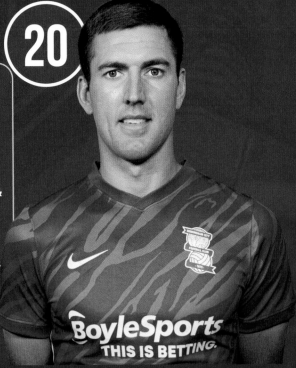

Birthplace:	**Solihull**
Birthdate:	**29 June 1992**
2020-21 appearances:	**25 + 12**
2020-21 goals:	**2**
Previous clubs:	**Aston Villa, Coventry City (L), Sheffield Wednesday (L), Brighton & Hove Albion (L), Nottingham Forest (L), Barnsley (L)**
International:	**England Under 21**

Joined Blues in 2019 after a loan. Packs a powerful shot like his brother and Technical Director Craig, a former Blues player. When the brothers played together for Birmingham they became only the second pair of Blues brothers to do so.

JORDAN GRAHAM

24

Birthplace:	**Coventry**
Birthdate:	**5 March 1995**
2020-21 appearances:	**41 + 3**
2020-21 goals:	**13**
Previous clubs:	**Aston Villa, Ipswich Town (L), Bradford City (L), Wolves, Oxford Utd. (L), Fulham (L), Gillingham**

Signed on a two-year deal in June 2021, this winger played for the Republic of Ireland and then England at youth levels. Last season he scored 13 goals and contributed nine assists in all competitions for Gillingham. Jordan has plenty of pace, is always eager to take on his man and get crosses into the box.

6

RYAN WOODS

Birthplace:	**Norton Canes, Staffordshire**
Birthdate:	**13 December 1993**
2020-21 appearances:	**42 + 4**
2020-21 goals:	**0**
Previous clubs:	**Walsall, Shrewsbury Town, Brentford, Stoke City, Millwall (L)**

Signed on a three-year deal in June 2021, Woods is a technically gifted schemer who Blues will look to unlock defences and also to keep possession. Players' Player of the Year at Brentford in 2016-17 and Supporters' Player of the Year the following season, he skippered Stoke City before spending the last season and a half on loan at Millwall under former Blues player and manager Gary Rowett, who had managed him at Stoke as well.

TAHITH CHONG

7

Birthplace:	**Willemstad, Curaçao**
Birthdate:	**4 December 1999**
2020-21 appearances:	**25**
2020-21 goals:	**1**
Previous clubs:	**Feyenoord, Manchester Utd., Werder Bremen (L), Club Brugge (L)**

On loan for the season from Manchester United, the Netherlands Under 21 international winger spent last season in Germany and Belgium on top-flight loans, playing against the likes of Bayern Munich and Anderlecht. So far he has played 16 times for Manchester United including a Champions League game against Paris St-Germain and was also on the bench for another Champions League fixture with Juventus.

JONATHAN LEKO

14

Birthplace:	**Kinshasa, DR Congo**
Birthdate:	**24 April 1999**
2020-21 appearances:	**16 + 19**
2020-21 goals:	**0**
Previous clubs:	**WBA, Bristol City (L), Charlton Athletic (L).**
International:	**England Under 20**

Capped by England at five different age groups, Leko grew up in Birmingham after coming to England when he was eight and made his Premier League debut for West Brom when he was only 16! The winger joined Blues in August 2020 for an undisclosed fee and is on loan this season with Charlton Athletic.

RILEY McGREE

18

Birthplace:	**Gawler, South Australia**
Birthdate:	**2 November 1998**
2020-21 appearances:	**8 + 7**
2020-21 goals:	**1**
Previous clubs:	**Adelaide Utd., Club Brugge, Newcastle Jets (L), Melbourne City, Charlotte FC**
International:	**Australia**

McGree is on loan from Charlotte FC until January 2022 when he is due to return to the USA for Charlotte's first MLS season. When playing in Australia he was nominated for the FIFA Puskas award for the world's most beautiful goal of the calendar year for a spectacular scorpion kick.

51

KYLE HURST

Birthplace:	**Milton Keynes**
Birthdate:	**20 January 2002**
2020-21 appearances:	**0**
2020-21 goals:	**0**
Previous clubs:	**MK Dons**

With Blues since July 2018, this left-sided midfielder is capable of the spectacular, most notably seen with a stunning half-volley that once snatched an FA Youth Cup victory over Barnsley.

RYAN STIRK

Birthplace:	**Birmingham**
Birthdate:	**25 September 2000**
2020-21 appearances:	**2**
2020-21 goals:	**0**
Previous clubs:	**None**
International:	**Wales Under 21**

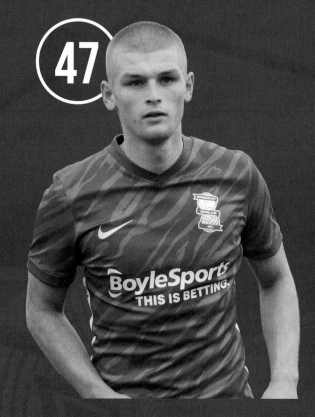

47

An FA Youth Cup semi-finalist with Blues in 2018, Stirk started against Cardiff City in May 2021 for his first team debut. Qualifying for Wales through his grandmother, the holding midfielder has won caps at four age groups.

TATE CAMPBELL

53

Birthplace:	**Birmingham**
Birthdate:	**27 June 2002**
2020-21 appearances:	**0**
2020-21 goals:	**0**
Previous clubs:	**Bromley (loan)**

Teenager who can be a commanding influence in central midfield; he scored twice in 15 Under 23 league appearances last season before spending the closing stages of the campaign in the National League on loan to Bromley helping them to qualify for the play-offs.

FORWARDS

10

LUKAS JUTKIEWICZ

Birthplace:	**Southampton**
Birthdate:	**28 March 1989**
2020-21 appearances:	**25 + 17**
2020-21 goals:	**8**
Previous clubs:	**Southampton, Swindon Town, Everton, Plymouth Argyle (L), Huddersfield Town (L), Motherwell (L), Coventry City, Middlesbrough, Bolton Wanderers (L), Burnley**

Their top scorer in 2020-21 with eight goals, Jutkiewicz first came to Blues on loan from Burnley in August 2016 and did so well the club invested a reported £1m to sign him permanently in the following transfer window. He scored 12 goals in his first season, six in his second, 14 in 2018-19 and 15 in 2019-20 when he was Blues Player of the Year. Going into this season Jutkiewicz had scored 112 goals in his career so far.

TROY DEENEY

36

Birthplace:	**Chelmsley Wood**
Birthdate:	**29 June 1988**
2020-21 appearances:	**19***
2020-21 goals:	**7***
Previous clubs:	**Chelmsley Town, Walsall, Halesowen Town (L), Watford.**

*2020-21 appearances and goals for Watford

Boyhood Blues fan Troy Deeney joined on a two-year deal 24 hours before the summer 21 transfer window closed. Despite being thought of as 'Mr Watford', after 11 years at Vicarage Road, during which he scored 140 goals in 340 + 79 games, Troy arrived at St. Andrew's already sporting a tattoo of the Birmingham City badge on his leg! Renowned as a strong, commanding centre-forward, Deeney has earned great respect throughout the country for his candid and honest interviews. He is a down-to-earth footballer who understands the fans and, being a Blues fan himself, is doubly determined to do what he did last season with Watford and steer the club to the Premier League.

CHUKS ANEKE

15

Birthplace:	**Newham, London**
Birthdate:	**3 July 1993**
2020-21 appearances:	**41**
2020-21 goals:	**16**
Previous clubs:	**Arsenal, Stevenage (L), Preston North End (L), Crewe Alexandra (L), Zulte Waregem, MK Dons, Charlton Athletic**

Capped at four youth levels by England, Aneke came through the Arsenal Academy and played for the Gunners in the League Cup. Three loans from Arsenal climaxed with him being a Wembley winner with Crewe in the 2013 Football League Trophy final before he moved to Belgium with Zulte Waregem in 2014. Three of his four goals in two seasons on the continent came in separate games against Mouscron before he joined MK Dons in 2016. 19 goals in his third season led to a move to Charlton and after 16 strikes in his second campaign last term he was added to Blues' firepower in June 2021.

SCOTT HOGAN

9

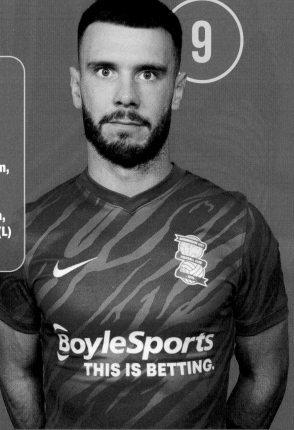

Birthplace:	**Salford**
Birthdate:	**13 April 1992**
2020-21 appearances:	**28 + 5**
2020-21 goals:	**7**
Previous clubs:	**Woodley Sports, FC Halifax Town, Mossley (L), Stocksbridge Park Steels, Ashton United, Hyde, Rochdale, Brentford, Aston Villa, Sheffield United (L), Stoke City (L)**
International:	**Republic of Ireland**

Capped eight times by the time the 2021-22 season started, Hogan has worked his way through a host of non-league clubs and has often hit patches of prolific goal-scoring, once being reported to have commanded a £9m fee when signing for Aston Villa. His brother Liam is a centre-back who he teamed up with at FC Halifax.

11 JEREMIE BELA

Birthplace:	**Melun, near Paris, France**
Birthdate:	**8 April 1993**
2020-21 appearances:	**26 + 9**
2020-21 goals:	**3**
Previous clubs:	**AS Herblay, Ville d'Evry, Viry-Chatillon, Clairefontaine, Lens, Dijon, Albacete**
International:	**France Under 16 / Angola**

Able to play on the right or left, or in support to the main striker, Bela scored Blues Goal of the Season in 2019-20 with a superb free-kick against Reading. Once a scorer against Wales for France at Under 16 level in October 2020, he also played for Angola against Mozambique. Mainly operating these days as a winger, Bela's work-rate makes him an important member of the squad.

CAOLAN BOYD-MUNCE

44

Birthplace:	**Belfast**
Birthdate:	**26 January 2000**
2020-21 appearances:	**1**
2020-21 goals:	**0**
Previous clubs:	**Glentoran, Redditch United (L)**
International:	**Northern Ireland Under 21**

A Blues youth product after starting with Glentoran, Boyd-Munce debuted against Portsmouth in the EFL Cup in August 2019, coming on as a sub for future England star Jude Bellingham. He appeared in eight first team games that season but just once in 2020-21.

ADAN GEORGE

40

Birthplace:	**Birmingham**
Birthdate:	**30 July 2002**
2020-21 appearances:	**0 + 1**
2020-21 goals:	**0**
Previous clubs:	**West Bromwich Albion, Bromsgrove Sporting (L), Walsall (L)**

Packed with pace and power, George joined Blues in 2015 and made his first team debut in the League Cup against Cambridge United, before coming off the bench in a home win over Brentford for his bow in the EFL.

KEYENDRAH SIMMONDS

54

Birthplace:	**Manchester**
Birthdate:	**31 May 2001**
2020-21 appearances:	**0 + 1**
2020-21 goals:	**0**
Previous clubs:	**Manchester City**
International:	**England Under 15**

Having been with his hometown team Manchester City since he was eight, Simmonds signed for Birmingham on 1 February 2021, making his debut at the end of the season against Blackburn Rovers. Earlier in the campaign he had scored against Lincoln City for Manchester City's Under 21s in the Football League Trophy.

ST. ANDREW'S

St. Andrew's has been home to Birmingham City since Boxing Day 1906, long before the word City was added to Birmingham's name! In fact when Birmingham moved to St. Andrew's they had only recently changed their name from Small Heath to Birmingham.

How many times have you been there?

How many times might you go in future, for as long as you live?

What is your favourite match there?

Here are some things about your footballing home that you might not know:

- The first game played there was a 0-0 draw with Middlesbrough on Boxing Day 1906. This top-flight match was watched by 32,000.
- The kick-off for the first match was delayed by an hour after hundreds of volunteers helped to clear snow off the pitch.
- Benny Green was given a piano for scoring the first ever goal at the ground. He actually scored twice in a 3-0 win over Preston North End, three days after the opening match.
- Birmingham did not play in the first ever FA Cup tie at St. Andrew's. That was a semi-final in March 1907 as Wednesday (later Sheffield Wednesday) beat Arsenal 3-1.
- During World War One (1914-1918) St. Andrew's was used by the army as a rifle range.
- The First Division title was won at St. Andrew's by Sunderland in 1936, when they beat Blues 7-2.
- The stadium's record attendance is 67,341 for an FA Cup tie with Everton in February 1939.
- In 1939 the ground was closed because the Chief Constable thought it would be a target for German air raids during World War Two.
- After questions were asked in the Houses of Parliament, the ban was lifted in March 1940 – but the ground suffered hits from 20 bombs during the war.

- In October 1941, England beat Wales 2-1 at St. Andrew's in a war-time international.
- In 1942, the main stand burned down – but it was an accident caused by the fire brigade who were using it as a base that caused the fire, not a bomb!
- Borussia Dortmund visited for the first match under floodlights in October 1956.
- In 1960, 17,000 watched South Africa beat a Midland Counties XV 16-5 at St. Andrew's in a rugby match.
- In 1961, Leicester City beat Sheffield United in an FA Cup semi-final replay. It was the ninth FA Cup semi-final to be staged at St. Andrew's.
- In 1972, Birmingham beat Stoke City 4-3 on penalties at St. Andrew's. It was the first ever penalty shoot-out in an FA Cup game.

- 'The Greatest' – Muhammad Ali – saw Blues play Liverpool at St. Andrew's in 1984. Major boxing bouts were staged at St. Andrew's in 1965 and 1949 when Henry Cooper and Dick Turpin retained 'British and Empire' titles.
- In 1987, Charlton Athletic beat Leeds United at St. Andrew's in the Play-off final replay for a place in the top-flight.
- In 1994, St. Andrew's began a major modernisation.
- In 2009, 18 miles worth of pipes were laid under the pitch to provide undersoil heating.
- In 2019-20 and 2020-21, Coventry City played their home games at St. Andrew's.
- St. Andrew's is the sixth highest league ground in Britain. It is 123 metres above sea level.
- The modern day, all-seated capacity is 29,409.
- The ground takes its name from the nearby St. Andrew's Church.

SPOT THE SEASON

Another test of your Blues knowledge! Using the clues provided,
do you think you can figure out what season is being described? Is it:

2013-14, 2014-15, 2015-16 or 2016-17?

1 Birmingham City finished 10th in the Championship for the second successive season.

2 Clayton Donaldson was top scorer with 11 goals.

3 Donaldson scored a first-half hat-trick in a 4-2 home win against Bristol City.

4 More games were won away from home than were lost.

5 Gary Rowett was Blues manager.

6 Northern Ireland international centre-forward Kyle Lafferty joined on loan from Norwich City.

7 The last home match of the season brought the highest attendance of the campaign when over 21,000 saw the game against Middlesbrough.

8 Michael Morrison played in every game.

9 Jonathan Grounds, Maikel Kieftenbeld, Stephen Gleeson and Tomasz Kuszczak all started at least 40 league games.

10 The best win of the season was a 5-2 win away to Fulham.

11 Diego Fabbrini was signed from Watford for a reported fee of £1.5m.

12 Leicester City won the Premier League and the two Manchester clubs won the domestic cups.

13 Burnley, Middlesbrough and Hull City won promotion from the Championship.

14 On the day the season kicked off Major Lazer and Justin Bieber were at Number 1 in the charts with 'Cold Water.'

Find the answer on page 61

BLUES GREATS
GIL MERRICK

Britain's best goalkeeper in the early 1950s.

Capped 23 times by England.

Played three times at the 1954 FIFA World Cup.

Famed for his tremendous positional sense.

Represented the Football League 11 times.

Blues record appearance-maker with 551 league and cup games.

Played 715 times for Blues in total including games played during World War Two.

715

Helped Blues win the Football League (South) title in 1945-46.

Conceded only 24 goals in 41 games as he helped Blues become Second Division Champions in 1949.

Won another Second Division title with Birmingham in 1955.

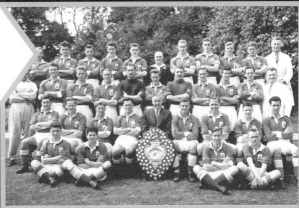

Played in the 1956 FA Cup final for Birmingham having conceded just two goals in five games as the final was reached.

Became manager of Birmingham City in 1960.

Led Birmingham to a European final against Roma in the Inter-Cities Fairs Cup in 1961.

Was with Birmingham as goalkeeper and manager from 1939 to 1964.

Won the League Cup as Birmingham manager in 1963 beating Aston Villa in the final.

The Railway Stand at St. Andrew's was renamed the Gil Merrick Stand in 2009.

Was inducted into the Birmingham City Hall of Fame and added to the Birmingham Walk of Stars in 2009.

BLUES WOMEN

Blues women play at the top level of the female game in the Barclays Women's Super League. Two exciting new signings for the 2021/22 season are both called Quinn: meet Lucy & Louise!

LUCY QUINN

Lucy has bounced back to Blues after two years with Tottenham Hotspur. One of 34 Barclays FA Women's Super League games she starred in for Spurs was the final game of last season – a match in which Birmingham secured their place at the top level of the Women's game.

In Lucy's first spell with Blues she played in 33 matches, during which one of her goals against Chelsea was voted Blues Women's Goal of the Season for 2018-19!

Although born in Southampton, it was with Portsmouth that Lucy set out on her football career which took her to Yeovil Town in 2016-17. Here, after a debut goal against Sheffield, she won promotion to WSL 1 before coming to Birmingham City for the first time.

It was also in 2017 that Lucy represented Great Britain at the World University Games in Taipei where she won the Golden Boot as top scorer. She spent six months studying in the USA at Wright State University in Ohio and studied for a degree in PE and Sports Coaching at the University of Chichester.

INTERNATIONALS

The future looks bright for Blues women who have several players making names for themselves as internationals.

Midfielder Christie Murray has broken into the Scotland squad and left-back Rebecca Holloway has earned recognition by Northern Ireland; while at Under 19 level, goalkeeper Elen Valentine, full-back Taylor Reynolds and central midfielder Sophie Phillips have all featured for Wales.

LOUISE QUINN

The summer arrival of defender Louise Quinn was a scoop for Blues Women! The experienced Republic of Ireland international excelled in Italy last season helping Fiorentina to finish fourth in the Women's Serie A.

Quinn's continental experience is not limited to Italy. After starting in her home country with Peamount United (with whom she won the Irish Cup) and University College Dublin, she moved to Sweden in 2013 and joined Eskilstuna United – in the home city of former Blues hero Seb Larsson. Louise helped Eskilstuna to promotion and on into the Champions League – a competition in which she once scored a hat-trick despite playing as a centre-back in her days in Ireland.

After her Scandinavian adventure, Quinn moved to England. Initially with Notts County she swiftly joined Arsenal. In 2018 she won the FA Women's Continental Tyres League Cup and added the Barclays FA Women's Super League title a year later in a season when she was named the Football Association of Ireland's Women's Player of the Year for the second time.

BLUES GREAT

These days, 144-times capped England international Karen Carney is most often seen as an excellent TV pundit. As a player she had two terrific spells with Blues; the first seeing her twice win the FA female Player of the Year award and also seeing Karen make her international breakthrough.

After representing Arsenal and Chicago Red Stars Karen came back to play for Blues in the WSL, UEFA Women's Champions League. She also scored both in the game and the penalty shoot-out as Blues won the Women's FA Cup in 2012, beating Chelsea who she went on to play for three years later.

Already a member of the Blues Hall of Fame, Karen has now also been inducted into the National Football Museum Hall of Fame. This is a fabulous achievement and one thoroughly deserved.

GREAT GAMES

QPR 3-4 BLUES
9 FEBRUARY 2019

A Che Adams hat-trick and a well-taken Harlee Dean goal had Blues 4-0 up before half time, but they had to hang on for victory. Boyhood Bluenose Matt Smith scored just before and after the interval for QPR and when Jordan Cousins made it 3-4 with 10 minutes to go, Rangers were rampant. When Steve McClaren's Hoops were awarded a last-minute penalty it looked like only one point would be taken after a 4-0 lead. Thankfully Lee Camp saved Nahki Wells' spot-kick to ensure victory.

BLUES 4-1 SPURS
1 MARCH 2008

Mikael Forssell's hat-trick was the high note of this taming of Tottenham in the Premier League. Having already beaten Spurs in London earlier in the season, Blues then completed the double over the Londoners for the first time in 32 years. With super-Swede Seb Larsson (still playing for Sweden in 2021) scoring a brilliant free-kick, Tottenham's last minute goal from modern day pundit Jermaine Jenas was just a consolation.

BLUES 4-0 WBA
18 DECEMBER 2004

Robbie Savage is best known nowadays as a TV and radio pundit but he got the ball rolling in this record-equalling win over the Baggies with an early penalty. Blues were three-up with just half an hour gone after goals from Clinton Morrison and Emile Heskey, both having been set up by Darren Carter. Birmingham stayed in control and nine minutes from time put the cherry on the victory cake with a late Darren Anderton free-kick.

STOKE CITY 0-7 BLUES
10 JANUARY 1998

Blues' best away win in the league was equalled in style as the Potters were smashed. Bryan Hughes scored in the 4th and 9th minutes to put Blues in command. Nicky Forster added to the lead before half-time, then after the interval, Birmingham ran away with the game with a second half hat-trick from Paul Furlong, followed by another goal from Jon McCarthy. It was simply too much for some of the home fans who had to be restrained at the final whistle by mounted police.

BLUES 7-1 BLACKPOOL
31 DECEMBER 1994

What a New Year's Eve! The Seasiders were rocked by Blues' biggest win in 35 years. It didn't look like that early on as Darren Bradshaw gave the Tangerines an eighth-minute advantage. It was Bradshaw's only league goal for Blackpool but he quickly got on the score-sheet again – scoring an own goal four minutes later. Louie Donowa put Blues ahead mid-way through the first half, then eight minutes before the break Steve Claridge smashed home a 30-yarder to make it 3-1. After half-time, further goals from Kenny Lowe and second strikes from Donowa and Claridge were capped by a late goal from George Parris, sending Blues into 1995 on a high!

BLUES 5-1 MANCHESTER UNITED
11 NOVEMBER 1978

Almost half way into November and Jim Smith's Blues had not won a league game, losing 10 of their 13 games including the last six. The visit of Manchester United looked daunting, especially after Joe Jordan gave the visitors an early lead, but Birmingham shocked everyone – probably including themselves! Half way through the first half Kevin Dillon brought Blues level and just past the half-hour point Alan Buckley scored twice in three minutes to sweep City into control. Whatever United boss Dave Sexton said at half time to revitalise his troops fell on stony ground as, just six minutes after the re-start, Don Givens scored against his old club to make it 4-1. That would have been a fabulous victory, but right at the death, Jimmy Calderwood made it even more special with a fifth.

ENGLAND'S FIRST CLUB IN EUROPE

Birmingham became the first English club to play in European competition once they got going in the mid-1950s.

Two English teams took part, with the other one being a London XI made up of players from various clubs; so Birmingham City were the first club to take part from this country.

The competition was the Inter-Cities Fairs Cup which actually lasted three years between 1956 and 1958!

Blues topped their group above Inter and a Zagreb XI.

Eddie Brown scored Blues' first goal in Europe and four goals in all, including two against Barcelona.

Blues played a Barcelona XI in the semi-final.

Barcelona were beaten 4-3 at St. Andrew's in the first leg.

An 82nd minute goal by Laszlo Kubala in the second leg made it 4-4 on aggregate.

Another late goal from Kubala settled a play-off game with Barcelona in Basel, Switzerland; the final score being 2-1.

Kubala went on to manage Barcelona and Spain. As a player he played for Spain but also Hungary and Czechoslovakia.

Barcelona went on to beat the London XI in the final.

Blues first game: 16 May 1956 Inter Milan 0-0 Birmingham City.

ENGLAND'S FIRST CLUB IN A EUROPEAN FINAL

When Birmingham reached the final of the second Inter-Cities Fairs Cup competition in 1960 they became the first English club to play in a European final – the London XI that had played in the previous final were a representative side not a club team.

Having played Barcelona in the semi-final in 1957, this time Blues met Barca in the final.

Over 40,000 came to St. Andrews to see the first leg which finished 0-0.

Harry Hooper scored for Blues in front of 75,000 at the Camp Nou but two goals from Zoltan Czibor and others from Eulogio Martinez and Lluis Coll gave the home side the trophy.

Birmingham also reached the Fairs Cup final the following season – this time losing 4-2 on aggregate to AS Roma.

What an achievement though for Blues to be the first English team in a European final - and then get to the final again a year later!

BLUES NEWS

Do you buy a programme when you go to see Blues at St. Andrews? If not, get one the next time you go. Match programmes give you all the official club news and provide great souvenirs of the games you have been to. Many people collect programmes. Rare ones often increase in value. They also provide you with a window into the world as styles and fashions change, as you can see from these programmes which go from way back in 1971 to 2004.

| **13 APRIL 1971** | V HULL CITY | RESULT: 0-0 |

This tall, thin programme had 24 pages and cost 5p. You could buy it with an extra little magazine called The Football League Review in which case it cost 7½p. Yes, there used to be ½p coins!

| **22 MARCH 1975** | V QPR | RESULT: 4-1 |

This 18-page programme cost 10p, twice as much as the programme from four years earlier.

| **9 SEPTEMBER 1978** | V LIVERPOOL | RESULT: 0-3 |

Manager Jim Smith was on the cover of this programme, which since the 1975 issue shown, had grown to 28 pages but had again doubled in price and by now cost 20p.

| **27 DECEMBER 1982** | V ASTON VILLA | RESULT: 3-0 |

By now the 28-page Birmingham City News programme included colour photographs. Previously the only colour picture had been on the cover. Once again the price had doubled since the last issue shown. The programme now cost 40p.

| **4 MARCH 1989** | V OXFORD UNITED | RESULT: 0-0 |

Compared to the 1982 programme against Villa, this edition had four fewer pages and the pages were smaller but the rising prices of the time meant the cost had increased again and by now it cost 60p.

27 JANUARY 1990 — V SHREWSBURY TOWN — RESULT: 0-1

This programme was a big improvement on the previous season's issues. It had increased by another 10p to 70p but by now it was the biggest Blues programme yet, seen with 32 pages.

12 MARCH 1991 — V FULHAM — RESULT: 2-0

There wasn't so much to read in this programme as the previous season although it had the same number of pages. The price had risen to £1.

15 FEBRUARY 1992 — V AFC BOURNEMOUTH — RESULT: 0-1

Louie Donowa was the Blues star on the cover of this 1992 issue that was the same size and price as the previous year's programme.

5 NOVEMBER 1992 — V BARI — RESULT: 1-0

This issue for an Anglo-Italian Cup game with Bari showed the programme continuing to rise in size and price, by now 40 pages and £1.20.

18 APRIL 1998 — V SWINDON TOWN — RESULT: 3-0

The programme for this season had undergone an upgrade in terms of ideas and design with a much more modern feel and some great features. By now it cost £1.70 but it had increased to 48 pages.

10 APRIL 2004 — V MANCHESTER UNITED — RESULT: 1-2

Mikael Forssell was pictured on the cover of this issue with the Barclaycard Premiership Player of the Month award. By now the programme had a thick card cover and cost £2.50 for 68 pages.

30 JANUARY 2018 — V SUNDERLAND — RESULT: 3-1

This packed, modern programme shows how programmes have developed over the past half-century. At 76 pages it was more than three times bigger than the 1971 issue featured here. On the other hand the price had increased over the years by 60 times from 5p to £3. If you want to be fully informed about your club though, Blues News is still a great way to learn about all that goes on at St. Andrews.

SPOT THE SEASON

One more test of your Blues knowledge! Using the clues provided, do you think you can figure out what season is being described? Is it:

1959-60, 1960-61, 1961-62 or 1962-63?

1 Birmingham City reached a European final for a second successive season.

2 Rather like in 2021 with tournaments like the Football League Trophy, the final was actually not played until the following season.

3 In the semi-final, Inter Milan were beaten at home and away.

4 Blues were managed by City Great Gil Merrick (see pages 40-41).

5 It was the first season of the League Cup and Blues' first game brought a win away to Bradford Park Avenue.

6 Blues reached the fifth round of the FA Cup, over 41,000 attending that tie at home to Leicester City.

 7 The double was done over West Bromwich Albion who were beaten at home and away.

 8 Blues were in the top flight, with Manchester United, Manchester City, Arsenal and Chelsea all beaten at St. Andrew's.

 9 Jimmy Harris was top scorer with 17 goals in all competitions.

 10 Goalkeeper Jimmy Schofield suffered a fractured skull in the home win over Manchester United.

 11 Tottenham Hotspur became the first team of the 20th century to do the double of winning the league and FA Cup in the same season.

 12 Three teams in the top flight scored over 100 goals and two teams conceded over 100.

13 On the day the season kicked off Cliff Richard and The Shadows were at Number 1 in the charts with 'Please Don't Tease.'

Find the answer on page 61

BLUES GREATS
BOB LATCHFORD

Won 12 caps for England, scoring five goals.

Scored 84 goals in 194 games for Birmingham City.

Won promotion in 1972.

Scored two hat-tricks as part of 27 league and cup goals in his promotion season.

Played for Blues in the FA Youth Cup final in 1967.

Scored Blues 100th hat-trick in a 4-1 win over Watford in 1971.

Scored in six successive Blues games in 1971.

Had two brothers who were goalkeepers: Dave for Blues and Peter for West Brom and Celtic.

Bob once went in goal for Blues when Gary Sprake was injured before half time as Wolves were beaten in 1973.

Was valued at a British record £350,000 when sold to Everton in 1974.

Howard Kendall and Archie Styles came to St. Andrew's as part of the deal that took Latchford to Goodison.

Became Everton's record post-war scorer.

Scored 30 top-flight goals in 1977-78.

Also played for Brisbane Lions, Swansea City, NAC Breda, Coventry City, Lincoln City, Newport County and Merthyr Tydfil.

Returned to St. Andrew's to work in the commercial department before becoming a coach in 1999-2000.

GOLDEN GOAL

Penalty shoot-outs are used these days to settle games where teams can't be separated. Back in the day, cup ties would sometimes go to several replays if teams kept drawing despite extra-time.

Penalty shoot-outs bring drama but are in some ways an unsatisfactory conclusion because while penalties are a skill, it is a skill isolated from the rest of the game. In 1993 the football authorities experimented with something called the Golden Goal.

- The idea of the Golden Goal was that whoever scored the first goal in extra time would win and the goal would be called the Golden Goal.
- It was just like a game of 'Next goal wins'.
- Penalty shoot-outs still existed if no goals were scored in extra-time.
- The finals of Euro 96 and Euro 2000 were decided on Golden Goals.
- In Euro 96 at Wembley, Oliver Bierhoff scored a 95th minute Golden Goal to help Germany beat the Czech Republic.
- In the Euro 2000 final in Rotterdam, David Trezeguet scored a Golden Goal in the 103rd minute as France defeated Italy.
- When France won the FIFA World Cup in 1998 they needed a Golden Goal to beat Paraguay in the second round.
- The Golden Goal was used between 1993 and 2004 but then abandoned.

BLUES GOLD

Birmingham City scored Wembley's first Golden Goal!

- Paul Tait scored with a header in the 103rd minute at Wembley as Birmingham City beat Carlisle United.

- The occasion was the 1995 Football League Trophy final; then called the Auto Windscreens Shield.

- 77,000 fans saw the goal after the 90 minutes had finished goalless.

- Birmingham were Wembley winners and history makers!

SECOND HALF OF THE SEASON

Hopefully Blues will be focussed on the top half of the table with a promotion or Play-off push in mind. They are all worth three points, so every match matters, but these five fixtures are special ones to look forward to:

1 JANUARY 2022
QUEENS PARK RANGERS H

2022 gets off to a great start with a visit from Queens Park Rangers. Blues have a good record against the Hoops with 24 league wins to QPR's 17 at the start of the season. Goals in the last ten minutes from Kristian Pedersen and Alen Halilovic dramatically turned a 0-1 score-line into a late 2-1 win when QPR came to St. Andrew's last term.

5 FEBRUARY 2022
SHEFFIELD UNITED H

Newly relegated from the Premier League and with former Chelsea player and Fulham manager Slavisa Jokanovic taking over to begin a new era at Bramall Lane, Sheffield will be looking to bounce straight back to the top level where they did so well two years ago. Going into the start of the season, Blues were unbeaten against the Blades since 2009, but this match should be a real test and one of the most attractive games of the campaign.

2 APRIL 2022
WEST BROMWICH ALBION H

Two goals from Gary McSheffrey sealed victory last time Blues beat the Baggies at St. Andrews, but that was back in 2006 so a home win in this derby is overdue and hopefully this time Blues can come out on top. For many this is the biggest game of the season and if a Bluenose can notch the winner, he is guaranteed to make himself a hero!

15 APRIL 2022
COVENTRY CITY H

Coventry City will feel an away game at Birmingham is a home from home after Blues helped The Sky Blues out by allowing them to play their home games at the St. Andrew's Stadium for the last two seasons. After winning promotion here in 2020 and staying up in 2021, they are now back in Coventry but will be on familiar turf when they return. All four games in the Championship and FA Cup while Coventry were Birmingham's tenants were drawn, with Blues winning the cup replay on penalties.

BLACKBURN ROVERS H

The last game of the season could have a lot at stake. If so, it will be a tense affair in one of the longest established fixtures in Blues history. The sides first met in the league way back in 1895 when Blackburn beat Blues 9-1! There have been many big score-lines in this fixture since, including a 7-5, a 7-1, a couple of 4-4 draws and even a 5-5 draw. If either team have won this season's first meeting a week before Christmas then victory in this match would register their 50th win in the head-to-head record.

Sky Bet Championship 2021/2022 fixtures

Day	Date	Club	H/A	Day	Date	Club	H/A
Sat	Aug 7	Sheffield United	A	Sun	Dec 26	Fulham	A
Sat	Aug 14	Stoke City	H	Wed	Dec 29	Peterborough United	H
Wed	Aug 18	A.F.C. Bournemouth	H	Sat	Jan 1	Queens Park Rangers	H
Sat	Aug 21	Luton Town	A	Sat	Jan 15	Preston North End	A
Sat	Aug 28	Barnsley	A	Sat	Jan 22	Barnsley	H
Sat	Sep 11	Derby County	H	Sat	Jan 29	Derby County	A
Wed	Sep 15	Fulham	H	Sat	Feb 5	Sheffield United	H
Sat	Sep 18	Peterborough United	A	Wed	Feb 9	A.F.C. Bournemouth	A
Sat	Sep 25	Preston North End	H	Sat	Feb 12	Luton Town	H
Tue	Sep 28	Queens Park Rangers	A	Sat	Feb 19	Stoke City	A
Sat	Oct 2	Nottingham Forest	H	Tue	Feb 22	Reading	A
Sat	Oct 16	West Bromwich Albion	A	Sat	Feb 26	Huddersfield Town	H
Wed	Oct 20	Huddersfield Town	A	Sat	Mar 5	Bristol City	A
Sat	Oct 23	Swansea City	H	Sat	Mar 12	Hull City	H
Sat	Oct 30	Middlesbrough	A	Tue	Mar 15	Middlesbrough	H
Tue	Nov 2	Bristol City	H	Sat	Mar 19	Swansea City	A
Sat	Nov 6	Reading	H	Sat	Apr 2	West Bromwich Albion	H
Sat	Nov 20	Hull City	A	Sat	Apr 9	Nottingham Forest	A
Tue	Nov 23	Coventry City	A	Fri	Apr 15	Coventry City	H
Sat	Nov 27	Blackpool	H	Mon	Apr 18	Blackpool	A
Sat	Dec 4	Millwall	A	Sat	Apr 23	Millwall	H
Sat	Dec 11	Cardiff City	H	Sat	Apr 30	Cardiff City	A
Sat	Dec 18	Blackburn Rovers	A	Sat	May 7	Blackburn Rovers	H

Fixtures are subject to change.
Check **www.bcfc.com** for up to the minute information.

KEEP RIGHT ON TO THE END OF THE ROAD

At Manchester City, supporters sing 'Blue Moon', at Liverpool the club anthem is 'You'll Never Walk Alone', while if the fans are singing, 'I'm Forever Blowing Bubbles' you know you are at West Ham. At Birmingham City the song, 'Keep Right On to the End of the Road' has been the club anthem since all the way back to 1956.

Blues reached the FA Cup final that year when the song became the soundtrack of the cup run. After beating Torquay United by a magnificent 7-1 away from home in the third round, it was on the way to Leyton Orient at the next stage that winger Alex Govan led the players on the team bus with a rendition of 'Keep Right On to the End of the Road.' After that match was won 4-0 and the fifth round produced a 1-0 victory over West Bromwich Albion at the Hawthorns, everyone hoped for a home draw at last.

Instead, Blues were handed a tough draw away to Arsenal. Once again Govan got everyone singing and when Blues fans heard the players singing, 'Keep Right On' as their coach arrived at the Gunners' old ground of Highbury, the supporters joined in. With Blues winning that afternoon by 3-1 to reach the semi-final, the song summed up the excitement of the cup run. This only strengthened after Sunderland were beaten 3-0 in the semi-final at Hillsborough and, while the Wembley final was lost 3-1 to Manchester City, by now, 'Keep Right On' was an essential part of a Blues matchday. In fact at the final in those days there was an official list of songs to be sung by the crowd and 'Keep Right On' was there to represent Birmingham.

Govan was Scottish, as was the song's writer and original singer Harry Lauder (or Sir Henry Lauder to give him his formal title). Almost half a century before his song was taken up by Blues, Lauder was such a big star that in 1911 he was the highest paid performer on the planet and became the first British artist to sell a million records. Sadly three days after Christmas in 1916, his only son, John C. Lauder, a captain in the 8th Argyll & Sutherland Highlanders, was killed at the Battle of the Somme - one of the biggest battles of World War One. Afterwards Harry received a letter from a fellow officer of his son saying that even when dying Captain Lauder had ordered his men to 'carry on.'

So it was as a tribute to his son that Harry Lauder wrote 'Keep Right On' and even starred in a film of the same name 20 years before it started to be sung at Birmingham City matches. Harry Lauder died six years before Blues fans started singing it, but the song lives on: 'Keep Right On to the End of the Road' is the song that to this day tells opponents that Birmingham City will never give up.

ANSWERS

CAN YOU MANAGE?
Pages 6 & 7

BLUES BOSSES

Alex McLeish – **Scotland**

Pep Clotet - **Spain**

Lee Bowyer – **England**

WHO PLAYS WHERE?

Bloomfield Road - **Blackpool**

Craven Cottage - **Fulham**

The Riverside Stadium - **Middlesbrough**

The Hawthorns – **West Bromwich Albion**

The New Den – **Millwall**

EYE-DENTITY

 Lukas Jutkiewicz

 Jérémie Bela

 Jonathan Leko

 Neil Etheridge

 George Friend

INTERNATIONAL BREAK

Neil Etheridge - **Philippines**

Kristian Pedersen - **Denmark**

Ivan Sunjic – **Croatia**

Riley McGree – **Australia**

Scott Hogan – **Republic of Ireland**

WHO SCORED?

1. **Lukas Jutkiewicz**
2. **Scott Hogan**
3. **Seb Larsson**
4. **Nikola Zigic**
5. **Obafemi Martins**

SPOT THE DIFFERENCE
Page 12

FACT OR FIB
Page 13

1. **Fib**	11. **Fib**
2. **Fact**	12. **Fib**
3. **Fact**	13. **Fib**
4. **Fact**	14. **Fact**
5. **Fib**	15. **Fact**
6. **Fact**	16. **Fib**
7. **Fact**	17. **Fib**
8. **Fact**	18. **Fact**
9. **Fact**	19. **Fib**
10. **Fib**	20. **Fact**

SPOT THE SEASON

Pages 14-15 - **2010-11** | Pages 38-39 - **2015-16** | Pages 50-51 - **1960-61**